Frances Turnbull

Published by Musicaliti® Publishers
575 Tonge Moor Road, Bolton, BL2 3BN

Copyright © 2016 Musicaliti
ISBN 978-1-907935-70-1

All rights reserved. No part of this publication may be reproduced, stored in a retrieval system, or transmitted by any means, mechanical, photocopying, recording or otherwise, without the prior permission of the copyright holder.

Index of Songs

A Tisket A Tasket	23
Bell Horses	24
Bobby Shaftoe	20
Bounce High	17
Cobbler Cobbler	9
Doggie Doggie	15
G-scale	27
I had a Dog	21
Lemonade	25
Lucy Locket	14
Rain Rain	10
Red Rover	19
Round and Round	13
See Saw	12
See Saw Margery Daw	22
Snail Snail	16
Star Light	11
We are Dancing	18
Where are you going?	26

Guitar Basics

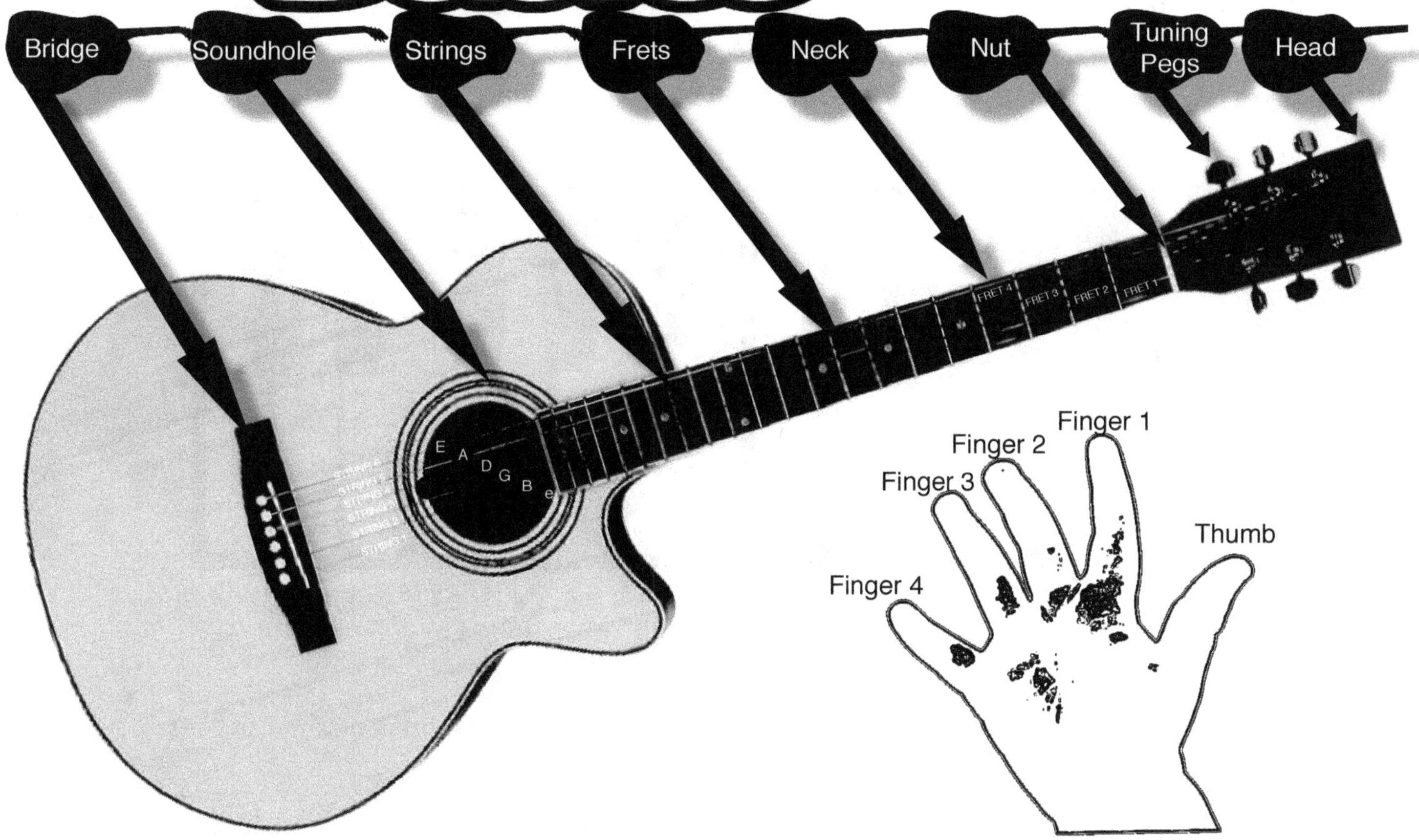

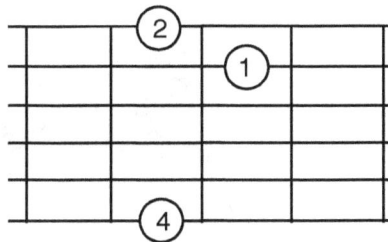
G chord

Guitar can be used to play tunes or **melodies** (one or a few notes at a time) or to accompany songs being sung - by playing all the strings with your fingers in the shape of a chord. The songs in this book are all in the chord of G. This means that you can play the G chord and sing along to the songs, or play the tune - it is a great skill to be able to do both! You could even have a guitar friend play the chord while you play the melody (tune) or the other way around! These pictures show the chords that we have used in this book. The numbers in circles show which finger to use!

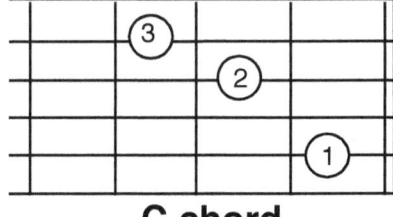
C chord

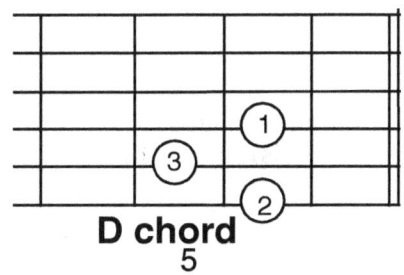
D chord

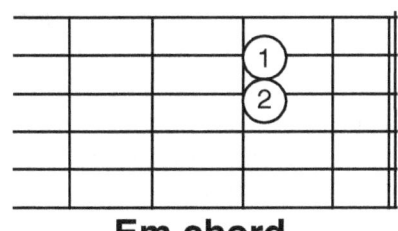
Em chord

How the notes work

The songs in this book are written in the **G scale**. Songs in the **green book** have the fewest notes as you get used to playing the notes of songs on the guitar, with more notes in **pink book**, **yellow book**, **blue book** and **orange book**.

The notes in a G scale are: **G, A, B, C, D, E, F#**. On a **piano**, they look like this:

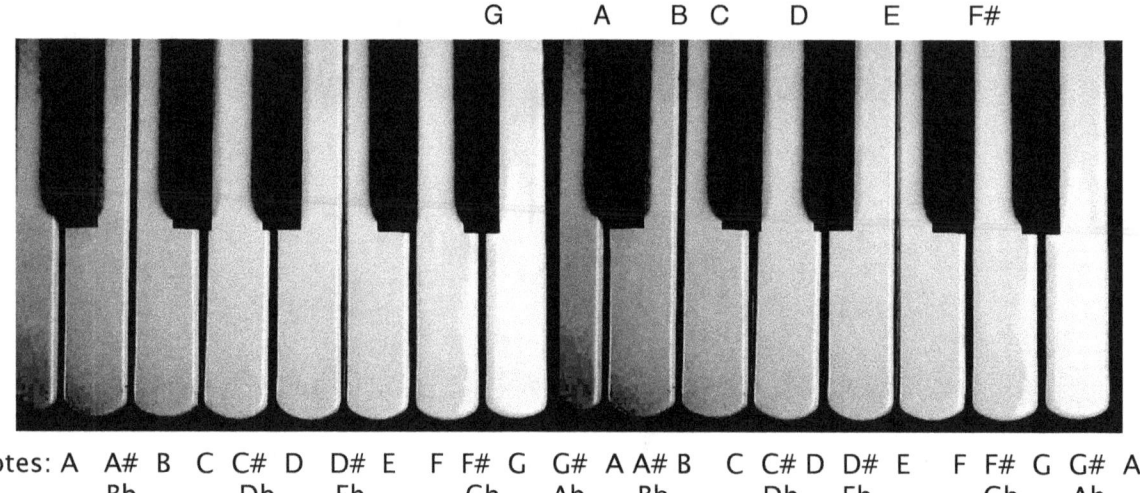

Music notes: A A# B C C# D D# E F F# G G# A A# B C C# D D# E F F# G G# A
　　　　　　　 Bb　　Db　Eb　　Gb　Ab　　Bb　　Db　Eb　　Gb　Ab

On a **guitar**, they look like this:
(guitar strings start with different notes/letters, and this picture shows the notes on the E string)

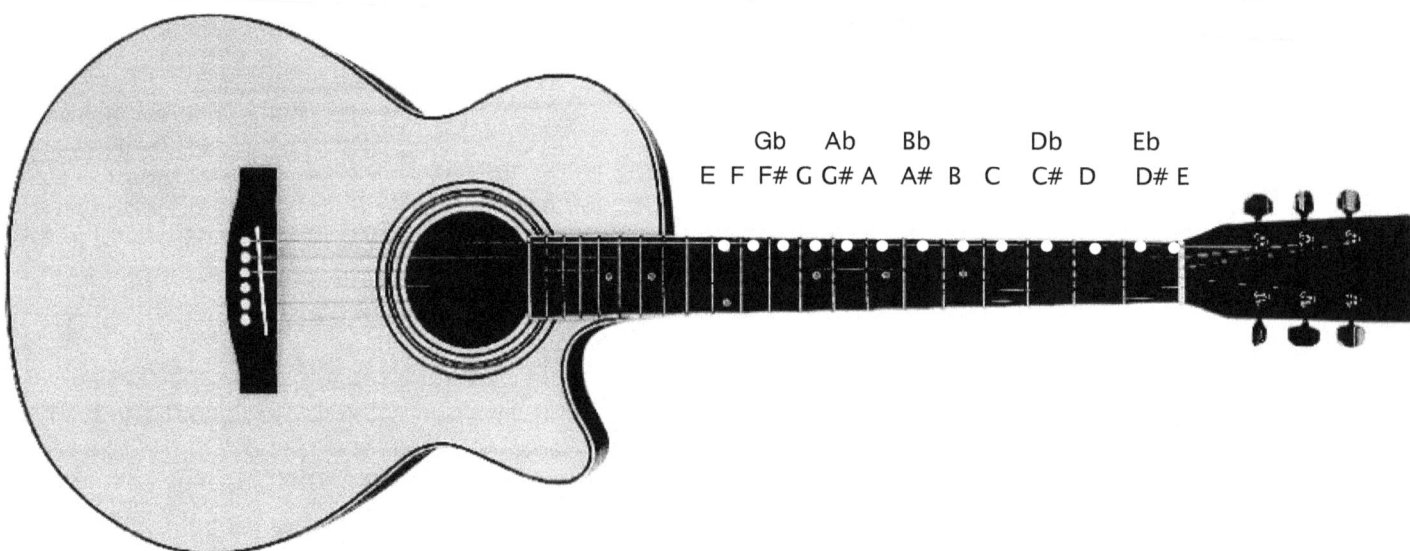

Scales have set gaps in between the notes, and the gaps between these notes determine when the black notes, or sharps and flats (also called accidentals) are used. Accidentals can be sharp (#) or flat (b), depending on the scale.

How the beats work

It's easy to focus on only playing the right notes, but we need to get the **long and short** beats right, too. It can be tricky to work out until we know what the lines and holes in the notes mean, so we can use **movement words** to remember how the beats sound. That way, you could say the movement words instead of the song words to remember how long to play the note!

Semibreve/Whole Note
VERY SLOW WALK
(4 beats)

Minim/Half Note
SLOW WALK
(2 beats)

Crotchet/Quarter Note
WALK
(1 beat)

Quaver/Eighth Note
JOGGING
(half of a beat)

Semiquaver/Sixteenth Note
JOGGING QUICKLY
(quarter of a beat)

***Dotted quaver-semiquaver /
Dotted eighth note sixteenth note***
SKIPPING
(short-long)

***Semiquaver-dotted quaver /
Sixteenth note dotted eighth note***
GALLOP
(long-short)

***Quaver semiquaver /
Eighth note-sixteenth note***
"HAMBURGER"
(slow-quick-quick)

***Semiquaver-quaver /
Sixteenth note-eighth note***
"SAUSAGES"
(quick-quick slow)

Repeat the part between these signs

For example, if we sang the movement rhythms to "This Old Man", we would have:

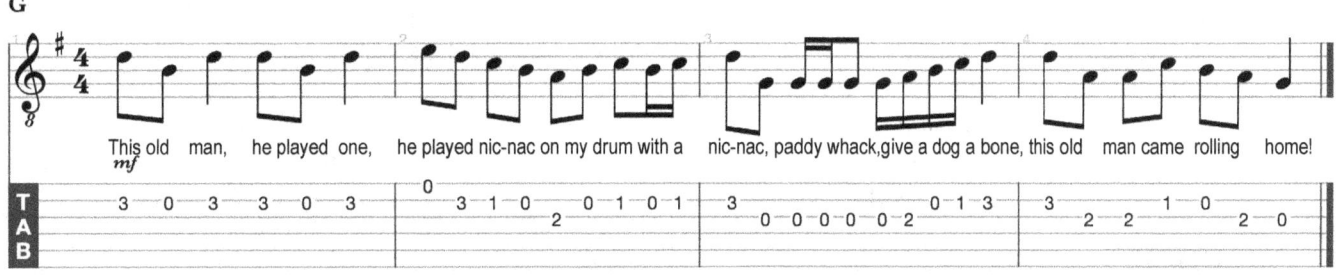

Give it a try before singing the songs!

These pages introduce songs with 2 and 3 notes, and the different lengths of beats used:

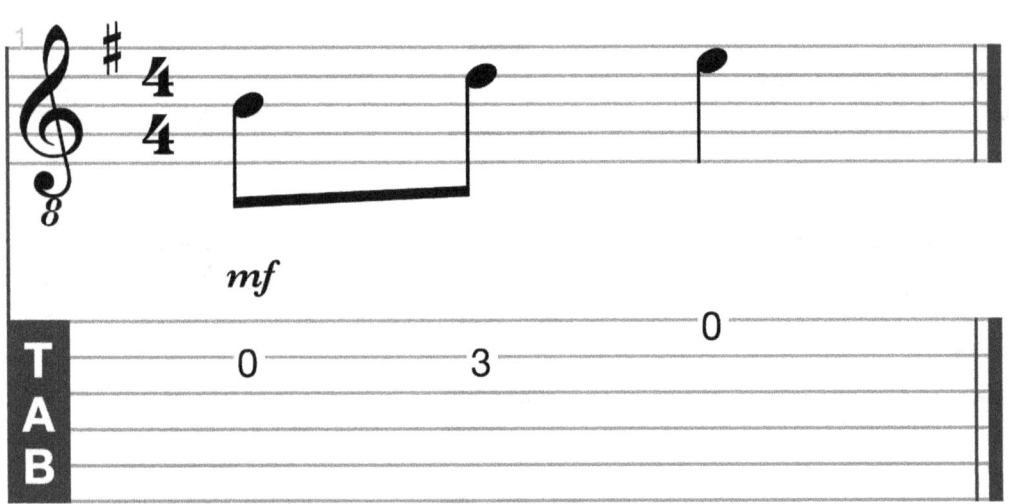

E is on the 1st open string
D is on the 2nd string, 3rd fret
B is on the 2nd open string

1st string
2nd string
3rd string
4th string
5th string
6th string

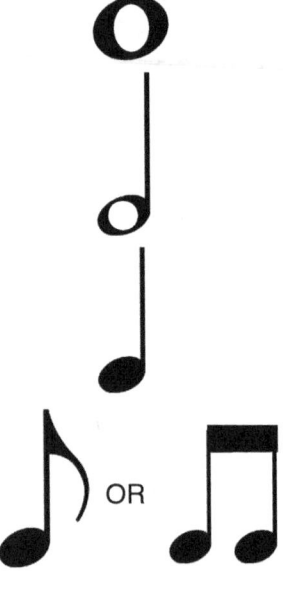

Semibreve/Whole Note
VERY SLOW WALK
(4 beats)

Minim/Half Note
SLOW WALK
(2 beats)

Crotchet/Quarter Note
WALK
(1 beat)

Quaver/Eighth Note
JOGGING
(half of a beat)

Semiquaver/Sixteenth Note
JOGGING QUICKLY
(quarter of a beat)

Dotted quaver-semiquaver / Dotted eighth note sixteenth note
SKIPPING
(short-long)

Semiquaver-dotted quaver / Sixteenth note dotted eighth note
GALLOP
(long-short)

Quaver semiquaver / Eighth note-sixteenth note
"HAMBURGER"
(slow-quick-quick)

Semiquaver-quaver / Sixteenth note-eighth note
"SAUSAGES"
(quick-quick slow)

Repeat the part between these signs

Cobbler Cobbler

Guitar Standard Tuning
E-A-D-G-B-E
♩ = 120

Traditional

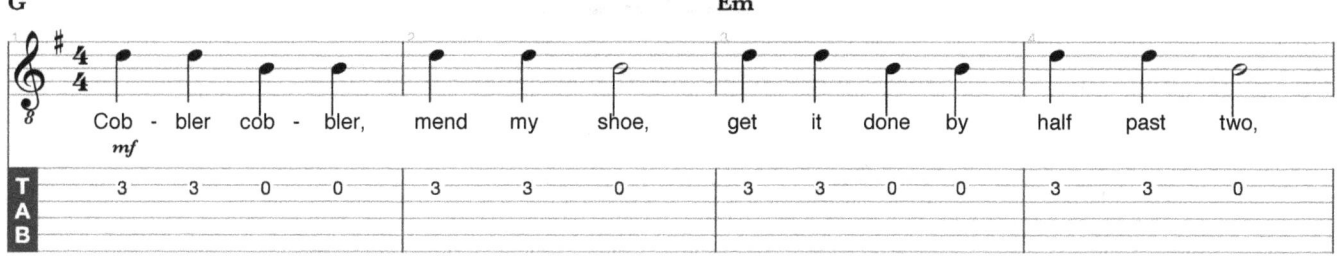

Cob - bler cob - bler, mend my shoe, get it done by half past two,

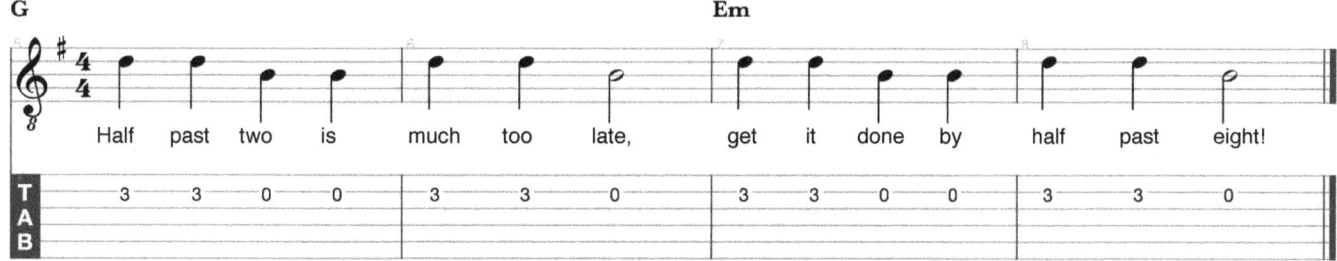

Half past two is much too late, get it done by half past eight!

Next verse:

**Stitch it up and stitch it down
And I'll give you a half a crown**

Guitar Standard Tuning
E-A-D-G-B-E
♩ = 120

Traditional

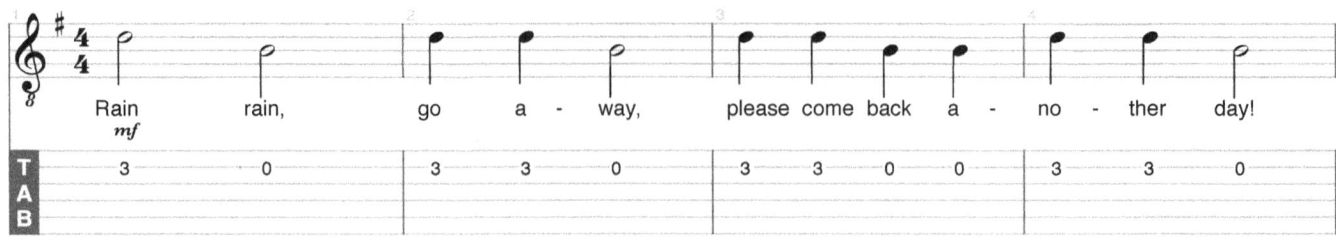

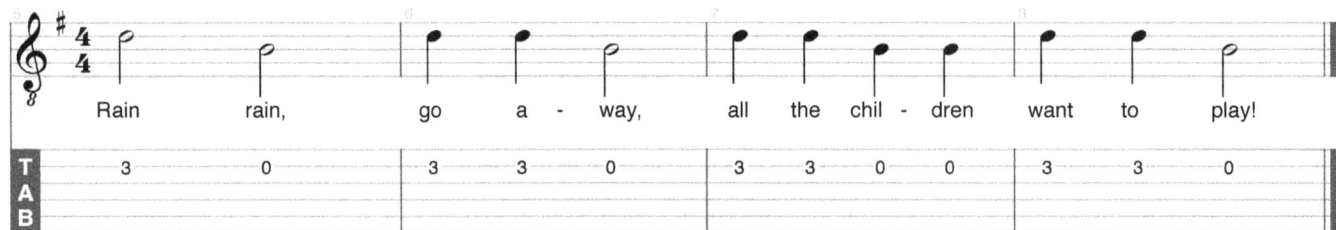

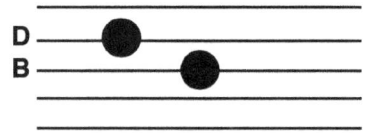

Guitar Standard Tuning
E-A-D-G-B-E
♩ = 120

Traditional

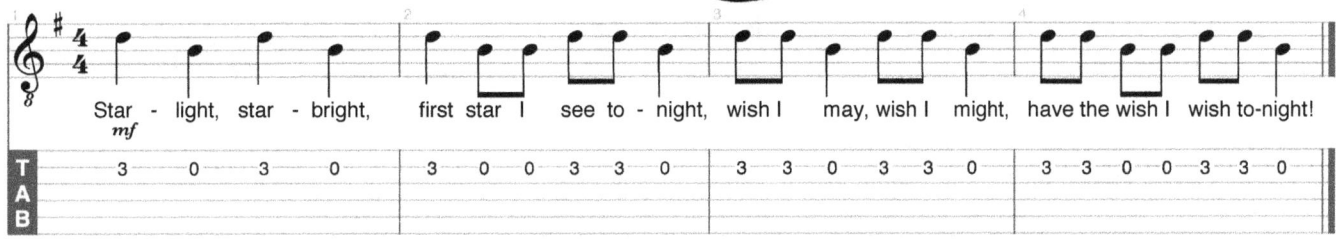

Star - light, star - bright, first star I see to - night, wish I may, wish I might, have the wish I wish to-night!

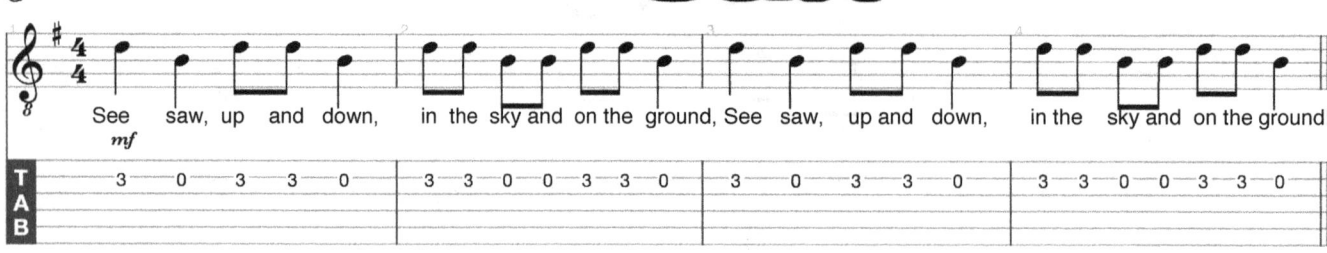

Guitar Standard Tuning
E-A-D-G-B-E
♩ = 120

Traditional

G

See saw, up and down, in the sky and on the ground, See saw, up and down, in the sky and on the ground!

  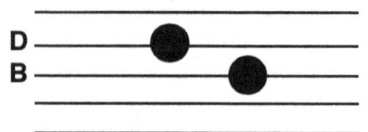

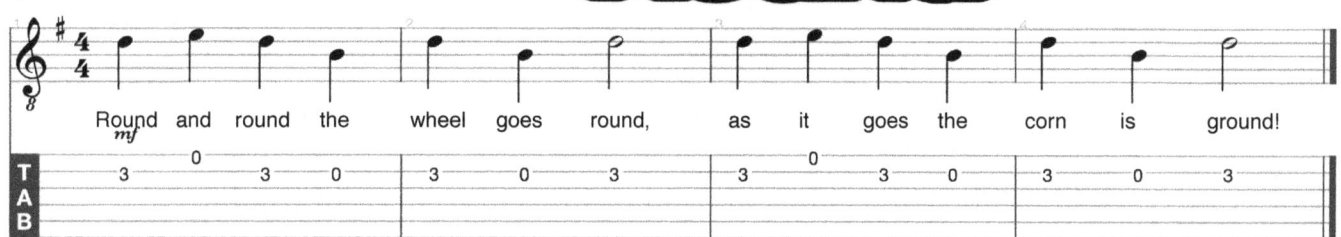

Guitar Standard Tuning
E-A-D-G-B-E
♩ = 120

Traditional

G

Round and round the wheel goes round, as it goes the corn is ground!

```
3   0   3   0   3   0   3   3   0   3   0   3   0   3
```

Lucy Locket

Traditional

Guitar Standard Tuning
E-A-D-G-B-E
♩ = 120

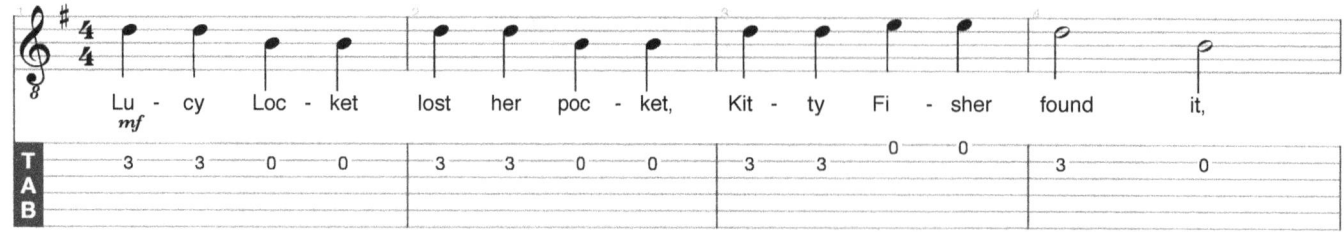

G

Lu - cy Loc - ket lost her poc - ket, Kit - ty Fi - sher found it,

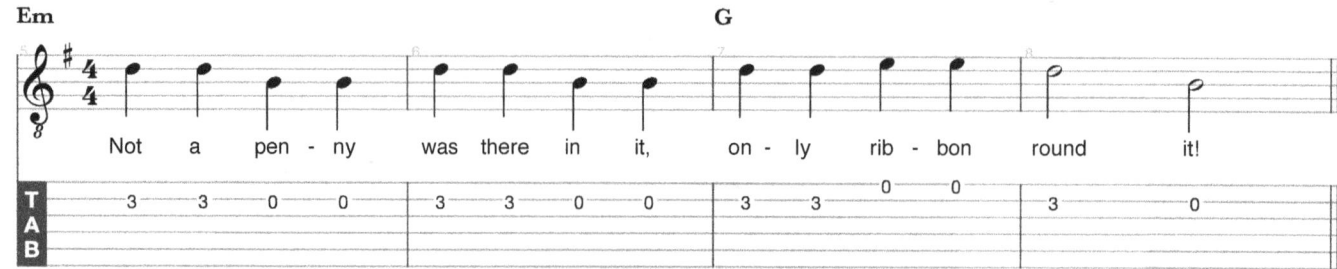

Em　　　　　　　　　　　　　　　**G**

Not a pen - ny was there in it, on - ly rib - bon round it!

Guitar Standard Tuning
E-A-D-G-B-E

♩ = 120

Traditional

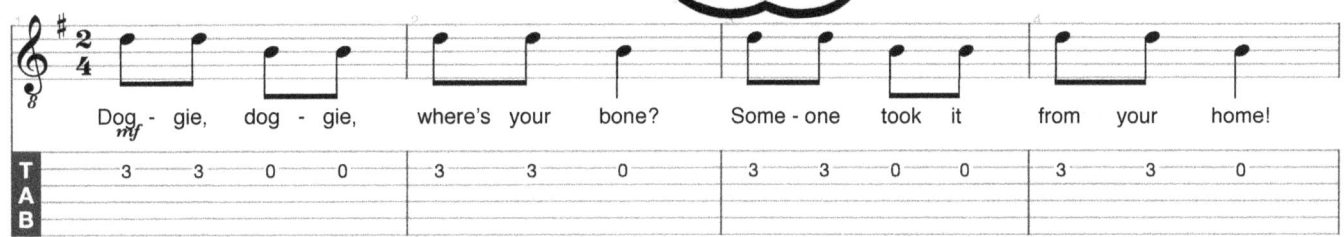

G

Dog - gie, dog - gie, where's your bone? Some - one took it from your home!

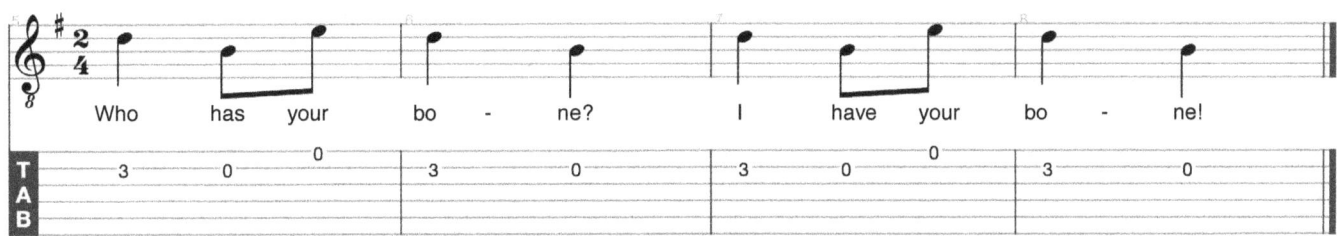

Who has your bo - ne? I have your bo - ne!

15

Guitar Standard Tuning
E-A-D-G-B-E
♩ = 120

Traditional

G

Snail snail, snail, snail, creep a - round and round and round!

Guitar Standard Tuning
E-A-D-G-B-E
♩ = 120

Traditional

Bounce high, bounce low, bounce the ball to Shi - loh, roll here, roll there, roll the ball to Leicester Square

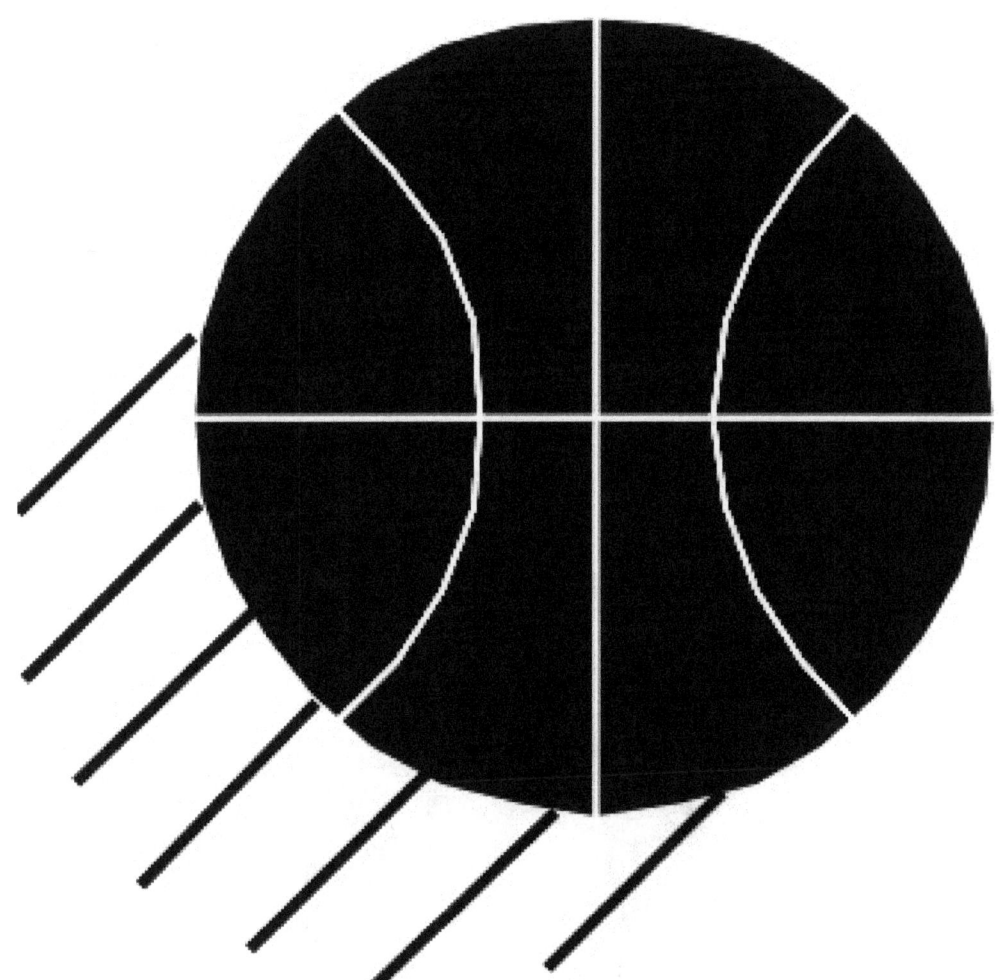

  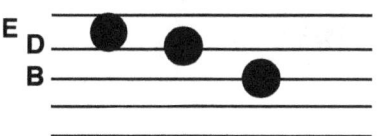

We are Dancing

Guitar Standard Tuning
E-A-D-G-B-E
♩ = 120

Traditional

G

We are dan - cing in the fo - rest while the wolf is far a - way,

Who knows what may hap - pen to us if he finds us at our play!

Next verse:

Wolf, are you there?
I'm combing my hair!
Wolf, are you there?
I'm coming to get you!

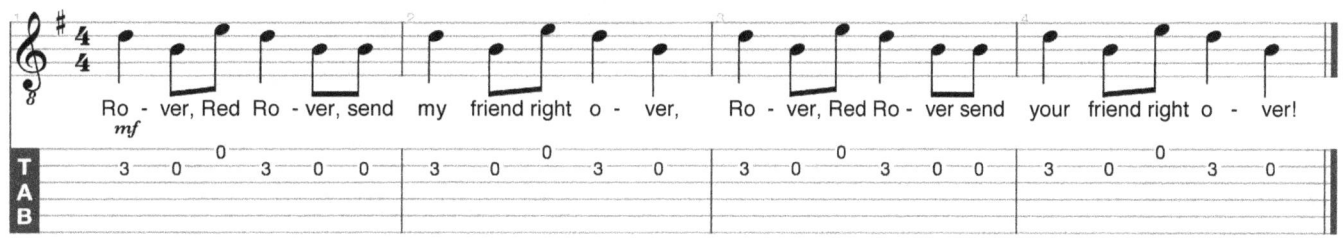

Guitar Standard Tuning
E-A-D-G-B-E
♩ = 120

G

Ro - ver, Red Ro - ver, send my friend right o - ver, Ro - ver, Red Ro - ver send your friend right o - ver!
mf

  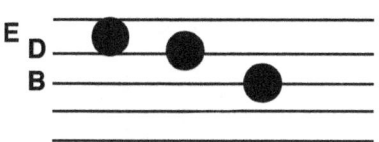

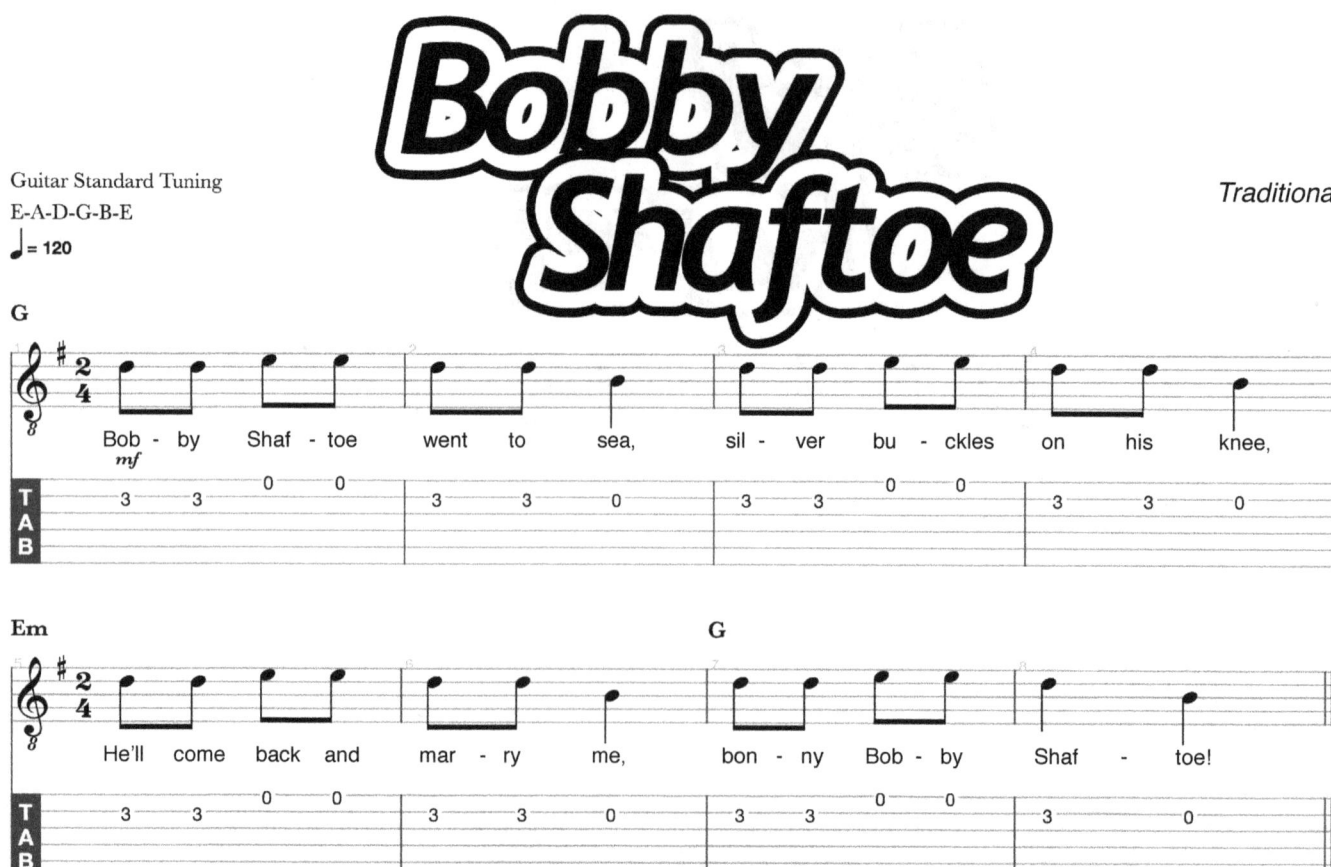

Guitar Standard Tuning
E-A-D-G-B-E
♩ = 120

Traditional

G

Bob - by Shaf - toe went to sea, sil - ver bu - ckles on his knee,

Em **G**

He'll come back and mar - ry me, bon - ny Bob - by Shaf - toe!

Next verse:

Bobby Shaftoe's fit and fair
Combing out his yellow hair
He's my love forevermore
Bonny Bobby Shaftoe

Bobby Shaftoe's looking out
All his ribbons flew about
All the ladies gave a shout,
Hey for Bobby Shaftoe

Guitar Standard Tuning
E-A-D-G-B-E
♩ = 120

Traditional

G

I had a dog, his name is Ro - ver, e-very time I called his name, he rolled over and o - ver!

Next verse:

**Roll over, Rover
Roll over, Rover
Roll over, Rover
Pass him on!**

See Saw Margery Daw

Guitar Standard Tuning
E-A-D-G-B-E
♩ = 120

Traditional

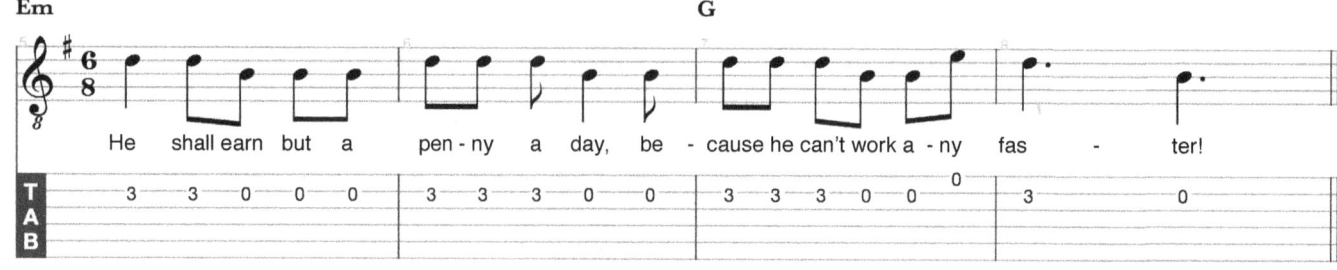

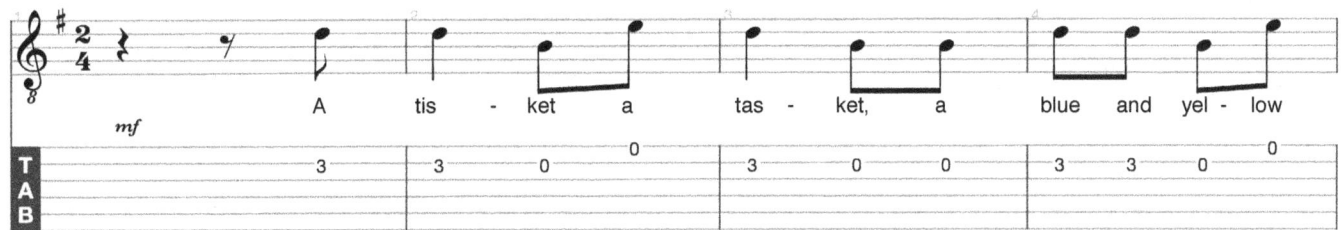

Guitar Standard Tuning
E-A-D-G-B-E
♩ = 120

Traditional

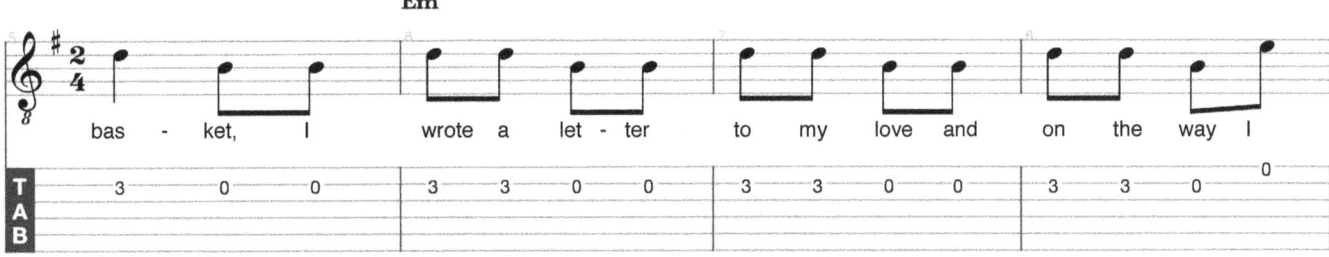

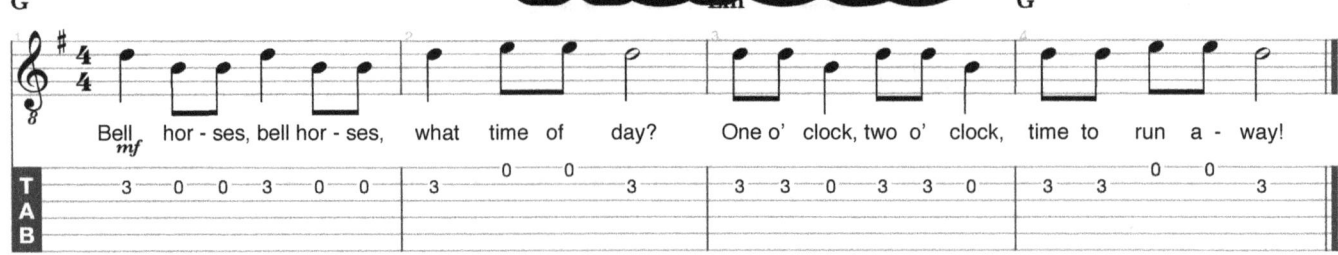

Guitar Standard Tuning
E-A-D-G-B-E
♩ = 120

Traditional

Bell hor - ses, bell hor - ses, what time of day? One o' clock, two o' clock, time to run a - way!

24

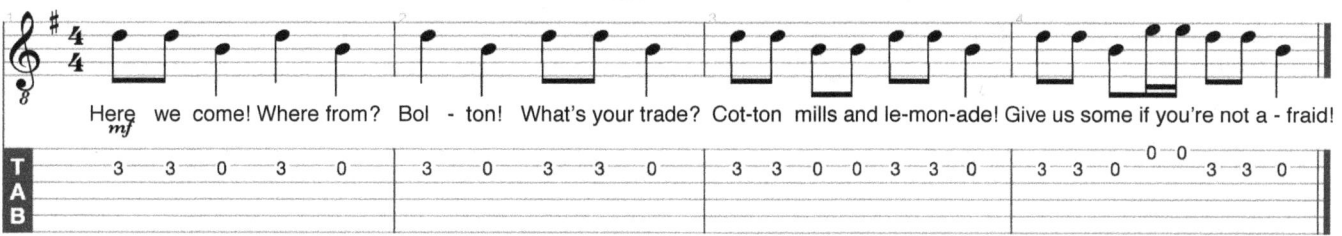

Lemonade Lemonade

Guitar Standard Tuning
E-A-D-G-B-E
♩ = 120

Traditional

G

Here we come! Where from? Bol - ton! What's your trade? Cot-ton mills and le-mon-ade! Give us some if you're not a - fraid!

mf

```
TAB:
3 3 0 3 0 | 3 0 3 3 0 | 3 3 0 0 3 3 0 | 3 3 0 0 0 3 3 0
```

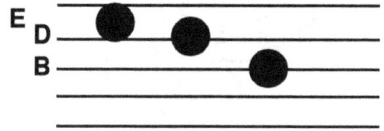

Where are you going?

Guitar Standard Tuning
E-A-D-G-B-E
♩ = 120

Traditional

G

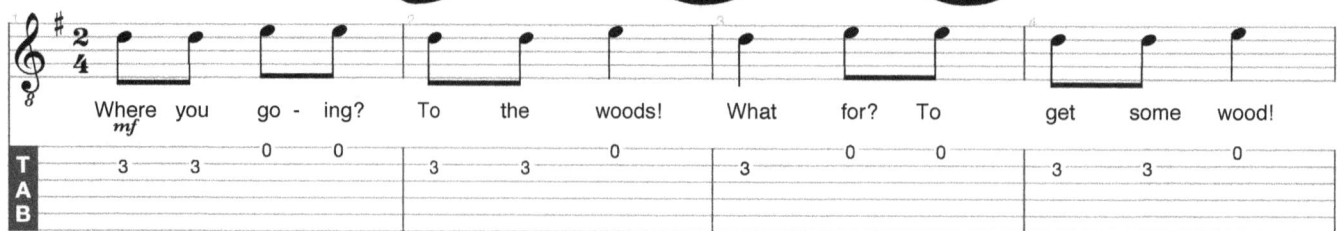

Where you go - ing? To the woods! What for? To get some wood!

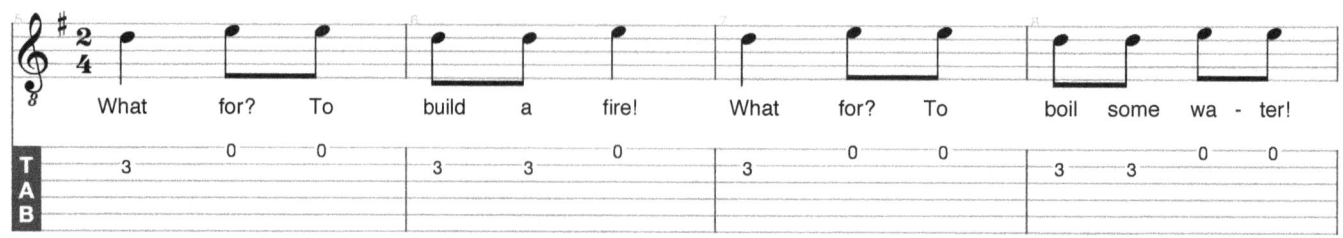

What for? To build a fire! What for? To boil some wa - ter!

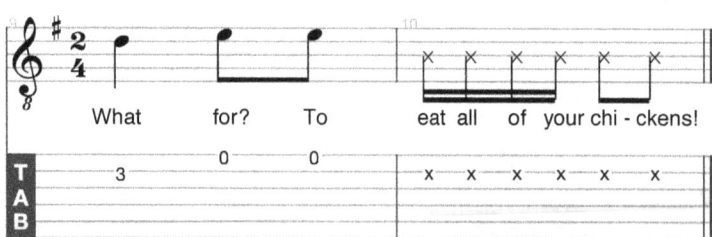

What for? To eat all of your chi - ckens!

E D

26

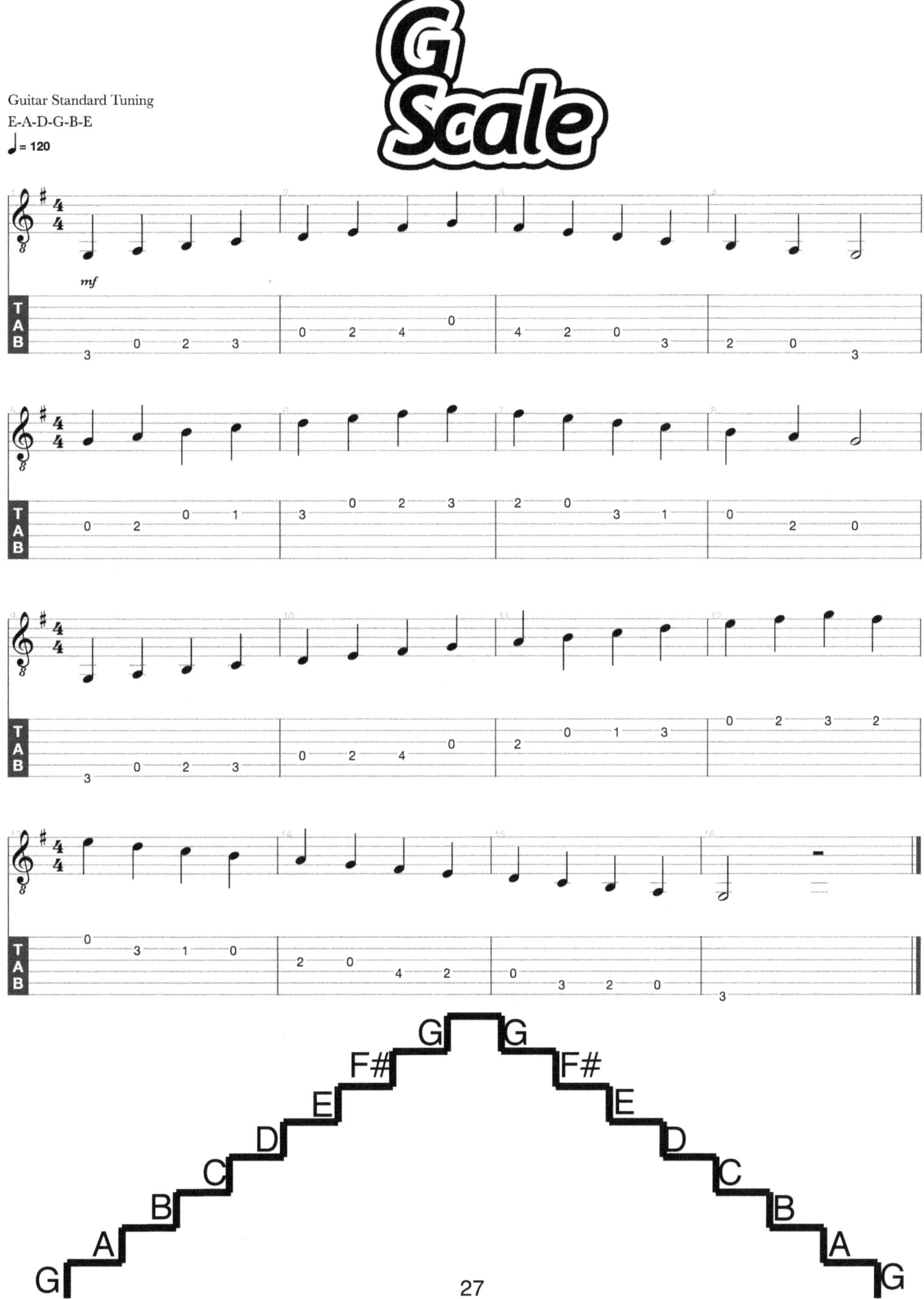

ABOUT THE AUTHOR

Frances has presented early years music sessions in a variety of settings since 2006, after training as a secondary mathematics and science teacher. She is fascinated by research into the health, educational and developmental benefits of music. Not content with being involved with children's music alone, she directs a local community choir, the Warblers.

AVAILABLE TITLES:

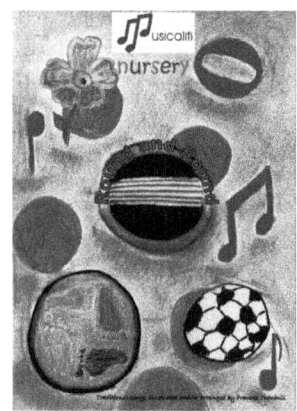

Musicaliti Nursery: Round and Round is a full-colour, illustrated book of well known children's songs for children. Each song includes music rhythms to which children can clap, tap, walk and sing.
ISBN: 978-1-907-935-008

Musicaliti Nursery Series: Magical Musical Kingdom is a full-colour, teaching series of well known and original children's songs with a royal element. Sessions include suggested instruments and activities, with an optional CD of music to purchase or download.
ISBN: 978-1-907-935-152

Musicaliti Nursery Series: Sharks, Fish, Shells is a full-colour, teaching series of well known and original children's songs with a fishy element. Sessions include suggested instruments and activities, with an optional CD of music to purchase or download.
ISBN: 978-1-907-935-169

Musicaliti Nursery Series: Yum, Yum, Yum! is a full-colour, teaching series of well known and original children's songs with a foody element. Sessions include suggested instruments and activities, with an optional CD of music to purchase or download.
ISBN: 978-1-907-935-206

Musicaliti Music Gone Wild is a full-colour, teaching series of well known and original children's songs with an animal element. Using ukulele instruction and chords, play along with your favourite animal songs today!

ISBN: 978-1-907-935-688

Musicaliti Goodies for Guitar is a full-colour, teaching series of well known and original children's songs for beginner guitar. With 90 songs both familiar and unfamiliar, this book covers songs in the scale of G, providing music notation, tablature and guitar chords for accompaniment.
ISBN: 978-1-907-935-206

FORTHCOMING TITLES:

Musicaliti Nursery Series: Balloons, Candles, Cake is a full-colour, teaching series of well known and original children's songs with a party element. Sessions include suggested instruments and activities, with an optional CD of music to purchase or download.
ISBN: 978-1-907-935-190

Musicaliti Nursery Series: Car, bike, plane is a full-colour, teaching series of well known and original children's songs with a transport element. Sessions include suggested instruments and activities, with an optional CD of music to purchase or download.

ISBN: 978-1-907-935-213

Follow Musicaliti **NOW on FaceBook, LinkedIn, ReverbNation, SoundCloud, Twitter and YouTube!**

www.ingramcontent.com/pod-product-compliance
Lightning Source LLC
Chambersburg PA
CBHW081503040426

42446CB00016B/3380